REALISM

ODYSSEYS

JESSICA GUNDERSON

CREATIVE EDUCATION•CREATIVE PAPERBACKS

Published by Creative Education and Creative Paperbacks
P.O. Box 227, Mankato, Minnesota 56002
Creative Education and Creative Paperbacks
are imprints of The Creative Company
www.thecreativecompany.us

Design and production by Blue Design
Art direction by Rita Marshall
Printed in the United States of America

Photographs by Alamy (Marion Kaplan, Visual Arts Library
[London]), Art Resource (The Metropolitan Museum of Art/
Art Resource, NY), The Bridgeman Art Library (Mathew Brady,
Honore Daumier, Heckscher Museum of Art, Huntington,
NY), Corbis (Geoffrey Clements, Hulton-Deutsch Collection,
Philadelphia Museum of Art, James Abbott McNeill Whistler),
Getty Images (American School, ROBYN BECK/AFP, Gustave
Courbet, Honore Daumier, Delacroix, Albrecht Durer, Thomas
Cowperthwait Eakins, Grant Faint, Winslow Homer, Imagno,
Albert Kaplan, Edouard Manet, Sir John Everett Millais, Jean-
Francois Millet, Pierre Petit/Hulton Archive, Pierson, Ilya
Efimovich Repin, Dante Gabriel Rossetti, T. Rowlandson, Jean
Baptiste Sabatier-Blot/George Eastman House, Time Life
Pictures/Mansell/Time Life Pictures, James Abbott McNeill
Whistler)

Library of Congress Cataloging-in-Publication Data
Gunderson, Jessica.
Realism / Jessica Gunderson.
p. cm. — (Odysseys in art)
Summary: An examination of the art movement known as
Realism from its beginnings in the mid-1800s to its decline in
the late 1800s, including an introduction to great artists and
works.
Includes bibliographical references and index.
ISBN 978-1-60818-535-1 (hardcover)
ISBN 978-1-62832-136-4 (pbk)
1. Realism in art—Juvenile literature. I. Title.

N6465.R4G86 2015
709.03'43—dc23   2014041724

CCSS: RI.8.1, 2, 3, 4; RI.9-10.1, 2, 3, 4; RI.11-12.1, 2, 3, 4

First Edition HC 9 8 7 6 5 4 3 2 1
First Edition PBK 9 8 7 6 5 4 3 2 1

Cover: *Study for the Cello Player* by Thomas Eakins (1896)
Page 2: *Joan of Arc Kissing the Sword of Deliverance* by Dante
Gabriel Rossetti (1863)
Pages 4–5: *Emperor Maximilian I* by Albrecht Dürer (1519)
Page 6: *The Fifer* by Edouard Manet (1866)

CONTENTS

Introduction

The history of the world can be told through accounts of great battles, the lives of kings and queens, and the discoveries and inventions of scientists and explorers. But the history of the way people think and feel about themselves and the world is told through art. From paintings of the hunt in prehistoric caves, to sacred art in the European Middle Ages, to the abstract forms of the 20th

OPPOSITE: Realist painter Gustave Courbet's early works, such as 1844's *The Happy Lovers*, show his reliance upon the established masters and Romantic ideals.

century, movements in art are the expression of a culture. Sometimes that expression is so powerful and compelling that it reaches through time to carry its message to another generation.

In the 19th century, Paris, France, was the artistic center of the world, and the exhibitions held there set the stage for trends in art. At the 1850–51 Paris Salon, spectators gathered around three large paintings by French artist Gustave Courbet (1819–77). The subjects of the paintings were poor, ordinary **peasants** and working-class people. The crowd stirred in agitation. Peasants were improper subjects for art. They were not to be admired. They were not beautiful. And Courbet's paintings, the crowd agreed, were ugly. But by Courbet's work, the confines of tradition had been loosened. A new light shone upon the working class and illuminated the realities of life.

The Rise of Realism

The **Industrial Revolution** swept
across Europe and much of the
world from the mid-18th to the
early 19th century, bringing with
it advancements in technology
that caused social, cultural, and
economic changes in many
countries. The development of the
steam locomotive in 1804 led to
quicker and easier transportation.
Soon, railroads snaked across

Great Britain and other countries. Steam-driven machines replaced handheld tools. Factories that produced iron, steel, and wool sprang up in cities across Europe and the United States. The factories employed thousands of workers, and urban populations exploded.

As rural dwellers moved to cities for factory employment, the urban working class grew in number. The conditions for the workers were not always good, though. Factories employed women and children as well as men, and most workers had to labor for long hours at a low wage. As the gap between the upper class, which controlled the factories, and the working class widened, some scholars and **philosophers** focused their attention on the plight of the working class. Two German philosophers in particular would change the political, social, and economic ideas of the world forever: Friedrich Engels and Karl Marx.

Marx and Engels believed that one class could rule for only so long until another class took over. Eventually, this class struggle would result in a form of **socialism** called communism, a classless society in which all land, houses, and businesses belong to the people, and profits are shared by everyone. Together, Marx and Engels wrote *The Communist Manifesto* in 1848. The book had a widespread impact, stirring up socialist revolutions in cities such as Paris, France; Vienna, Austria; Berlin, Germany; and Milan and Venice, Italy.

At this time, the world of art was in the midst of the Romantic movement. Romantic art was often historic, reminiscent of **medieval** times, and depicted real or fictional heroes, inner and outer demons, and treacherous landscapes. Romantic art was aimed at eliciting the viewer's emotions. Passion flared in every stroke of the brush. But as the working class grew in number and began to attract the notice of philosophers, some artists also shifted their focus to the common person. The French Revolution of 1848, in which Parisian workers overthrew the **monarchy** and established a **democratic** government, caused French artists such as Jean-François Millet (1814–75) and Gustave Courbet to look more closely at peasant life. In French art before 1848, ordinary people had been shown in only small, modest paintings, but Millet and Courbet sought to change that tradition with their large depictions of peasants.

The Revolutions of 1848

The Revolutions of 1848 were a series of revolts against European monarchies, beginning in Sicily and France and spreading to other countries in Europe and as far away as Brazil. The revolutions erupted from a variety of causes, including the many social, economic, and political changes that had taken place in the first half of the 19th century. Technological advancements changed the lifestyles of the working class, the press increased political knowledge among the masses, and new social theories began to spring up. Economic slumps and crop failures left the peasants and working class impoverished and were the catalysts for revolution in many countries. Although the revolutions were largely deemed failures, they did succeed in helping to unify Germany and Italy while also raising awareness of working-class conditions.

Another factor in the changing artistic focus was the emergence of a philosophy known as Positivism, which held that progress in human society could be achieved by close observation of the natural world. The second half of the 19th century became known as the Positivist Age, and the popularity of Positivist thought soon caused a widespread rejection of Romantic fictional subjects in favor of factual, ordinary subjects from the modern world. Art critics called this new, true-to-life style of art Realism.

Realists not only rejected Romantic subjects, but they disapproved of Classical Greek and Roman gods and leaders as subjects as well. They believed such historical **themes** were irrelevant to the present. Realist artists aimed to depict current events and ordinary people with as much accuracy as possible. They felt that only the things of their own time—the things they could see and hear and touch—were real.

Realism came into being slowly, as many artists began to combine aspects of both Romanticism and Realism. Spanish artist Francisco de Goya (1746–1828) worked mostly in the Romantic tradition, but his great work, *The Third of May, 1808* (1814), tells the story of innocent civilians who were gunned down by French soldiers during Napoleon's occupation of Spain. Goya made numerous studies of the area where the execution took place, and though his painting reveals emotion and passion in the Romantic sense, it also provides an accurate portrayal of ordinary citizens common to the Realist movement.

One technological advancement of the age that spurred Realism into a dominant movement was the modern camera. Although some form of the camera had

been in use for centuries, developments in the 19th century made it possible for artists to conveniently use the camera as a tool. In the 1830s, French artist and chemist Louis Daguerre (1787–1851) successfully developed a method of photography using copper plates coated in **iodized** silver to capture a permanent image, which he called a daguerreotype. Daguerre's invention prompted English scientist William Henry Fox Talbot (1800–77) to publicize his work on the calotype process, which became the basis for modern photography, as it produced an image from which duplicates could be printed.

Photography changed the art world dramatically. With the use of a camera, artists could capture an event the moment it occurred. Photographs recorded the real world in a truthful and accurate way and provided evidence that what the human eye saw was really there.

Now, Realists who longed to depict common, current experiences could do so with the release of the camera's shutter. But many traditional artists and critics posed a new question: Could this new way of representing the world be considered art?

Some artists answered no. They responded angrily to the rise of photography in art, worried that their skilled work at detailing paintings and sculptures was being replaced by a quick and almost effortless method. The art of painted portraiture was in the most

danger. Photographed portraits quickly became popular, as they were more affordable to the masses than painted portraits. When the daguerreotype method was released in 1839, French painter Paul Delaroche (1797–1856) exclaimed, "From this moment, painting is dead!" In a similar tone, French artist Maurice de Vlaminck (1876–1958) later declared, "We hate everything that has to do with the photograph." Try as they might, though, these artists could do nothing to stop photography from growing.

Part of the reason photography grew so quickly was that some artists embraced it as a helpful tool for painting. Instead of using a live model who tired after a few hours, they could paint from a photograph of the model instead. Others argued that photography was not just a tool; it was a new form of art. One of the first photos, Talbot's *The Open Door* (1844), of a rural English cottage, is considered a work of art by many.

In the U.S., Realism was also a rising tradition. When the American Civil War erupted in 1861, photographers from all over the country rushed to the battlefields, hoping to document the war. The most well-known of these was American Mathew Brady (1823–96). Brady and his assistants took more than 7,000 photographs of the war front. Their photos showed that war was not glamorous and heroic as artists had portrayed it in the past; instead, it was grim, horrifying, and deadly.

As the technologies of the world changed, so did society and the artists who depicted that society. Realism offered an investigation into the lives of ordinary people and events, and it eventually grew to include all classes of society, all types of people, and the environments in which they lived.

The American Civil War

The Civil War in the U.S. lasted from 1861 to 1865. Fought largely over the issue of slavery, the war pitted Northern "free" states against Southern states that allowed slavery. When Abraham Lincoln, who was against slavery, was elected president in 1860, seven Southern states broke away from the Union to form the Confederate States of America, and after war broke out in 1861, four more states joined the Confederacy. After four years of bitter fighting, the South finally surrendered in 1865. By that time, more than 600,000 soldiers were dead and many cities and homes in the South were destroyed. It took dozens of years for the rift between the North and South to be repaired.

The Artists of the Realist Movement

One of the leading artists of the French Realist movement was Gustave Courbet, who was born in the small French village of Ornans to a wealthy farming family. In 1847, Courbet took a trip to the Netherlands to study Dutch painters such as Rembrandt van Rijn (1606–69) and Frans Hals (1580–1666). The trip changed his views on art forever. He saw that

OPPOSITE: Never one to shy away from controversy—whether in art, politics, or any other arena—Courbet asserted his artistic independence at critical junctures throughout his career.

these Dutch masters painted the world around them rather than imagined or Classical subjects. Courbet took the idea to heart. He rejected the sentimentality and emotion of the Romantics in favor of a more realistic, factual style. All imaginative subjects were ruled out because they were not visible to the human eye. "I cannot paint an angel," he said, "because I have never seen one."

The French Revolution of 1848 also changed the approach Courbet took to his work. The Revolution had shone a light on the lives of the peasants and working class, and in response, Courbet focused on the poor and ordinary in his paintings. The detail and respect he gave his humble, ordinary subjects was something that had rarely been done in high art. When he was rejected from the Universal Exhibition of 1855, Courbet set up his own gallery on the grounds of the Exhibition, calling it the Pavilion of Realism. His artistic goal, in his words, was "to be able to translate the customs, ideas, and appearances of my time as I see them."

Jean-François Millet was another leader of French Realism. He grew up on a farm in rural France and at the age of 24 moved to Paris to pursue his art career. He soon drew away from the official, **academic** style of painting nudes and portraits and began to depict rural scenes. As with Courbet, the Revolutions of 1848 led Millet to focus on ordinary subjects. In his paintings, Millet depicted both the pleasures and the difficulties of rural life. He gave dignity to rural tasks such as sowing and gathering, deliberately leaving out technological farming advancements of the time and instead emphasizing simple tools, such as the rake and the hoe. Inspired by the social issues of the Revolutions of 1848, he depicted his peasant subjects as heroes.

Although in many cases French Realist artists chose to paint rural landscapes, one artist, Honoré Daumier (1808–79), chose to depict urban life. Daumier was a **lithographer** as well as a painter and made many lithographs for liberal French journals. In his lithographs, he mocked high society, illuminating the misbehavior of politicians and the middle class. He had much affection for the working class and often focused on social and cultural themes in his artwork. One such work,

Lithography

After German playwright Aloys Senefelder invented lithography in 1796, the process became popular with many artists, and it is still used today. To create a lithograph, an artist draws on a flat surface, usually stone, with a greasy substance. The stone's surface is wiped first with water, then with an oil-based ink. The ink sticks to the greasy drawing but not to the wet areas of the stone. Next, a sheet of paper is laid on the stone, and both the stone and the paper are passed through a flatbed press, which pushes the paper onto another flat surface. The ink is transferred to the paper, creating a printed image. Because the process can be repeated to produce duplicates, many artists, including Eugène Delacroix, Francisco de Goya, and Honoré Daumier, took up lithography.

Rue Transnonain (1834), served as a commentary on the unfair treatment of the working class by the French government and was painted in reaction to the massacre of the people of a working-class neighborhood after the killing of a civil guard during a worker demonstration. In this lithograph, Daumier shows the moments after the massacre. Lifeless bodies lie on the floor; one man is wearing his bedclothes. The realistic portrayal of the scene is objective and photographic, but the viewer need only look at the piece to feel compassion for the dead.

Rosa Bonheur (1822–99) was a female French artist who made great achievements in the male-dominated art world. Her parents believed in the equality of women, and her father taught her to draw and paint when she was a young girl. Even though she grew up in Paris, Bonheur did not like the city lifestyle. She loved farm animals and chose to paint oxen, horses, and pigs, studying them in great detail in order to portray them as accurately as possible. She went to horse fairs to view the animals in life, and she also went to slaughterhouses to see the animals in death. In order to move about freely, she often wore men's clothing when she went to the slaughterhouses, but she had to obtain police permission to wear pants. *The Horse Fair* (1853–55), one of Bonheur's best-known works, is lifelike in its colors and the detailed muscles of the horses. Bonheur became so famous that she was the first woman to be awarded France's top recognition, the Grand Cross of the Legion of Honor.

Realism began in France, but artists in other countries were considered Realists as well. The most prominent German Realist was Wilhelm Leibl (1844–1900). Leibl was trained at Munich Academy, and when he saw an

exhibition of Courbet's work in Germany, he turned to Realism. He went to Paris for a few years to study the art that was being produced there. Later, he moved to Bavaria, a rural area of southeastern Germany, where he focused on peasant subjects, illustrating their natural virtues such as simplicity and honesty.

Russian artist Ilya Repin (1844–1930), from a village in the Ukraine, began his career by studying portraiture and was later accepted into the St. Petersburg Academy of Arts. With financial aid from the Academy, he traveled to Paris and Italy. Upon his return to Russia, Repin joined the Wanderers, a group of painters who brought art to rural people through traveling exhibitions. Like the other members of the group, he rebelled against the formalism of the Academy and was drawn to the common people, frequently painting Ukrainian and Russian country dwellers. His famous painting *A Religious Procession in the Province of Kursk* (1880–83) shows peasants on a religious journey. Their poverty and misery are evident in Repin's realistic portrayal.

Repin rebelled against the formalism of the Academy and was drawn to the common people.

Winslow Homer (1836–1910), a leading American painter in the late 19th century, was largely self-taught and began his artistic career by making newspaper illustrations of everyday life. In 1859, he opened a studio in New York City and turned a fresh page as a painter rather than an illustrator. In 1862, he went to the battlefront to cover the Civil War. Rather than depicting heroic battle scenes, he focused his attention on the soldiers' lives behind the lines.

Although he lived in New York City, Homer took many trips to upstate New York. The quiet, rural lifestyle inspired him, and in 1870, he began painting scenes with a country setting. Often, he focused on the carefree past and the innocence of childhood. One of his most prominent works, *Snap the Whip* (1872), shows boys playing outside a one-room schoolhouse. His work charmed his urban, industrialized audience and sparked their nostalgia for a simpler life.

Even though it was discarded by many traditional artists, photography was the perfect medium for the art of the Realist movement. A French photographer who called himself Nadar (1820–1910) enthusiastically embraced the art of photography. He became interested in photography in 1849 as a tool to help him with a lithography project and fell so in love with it that a few years later he opened a photography studio. He avoided formal poses and encouraged his subjects to pose naturally and informally. An innovator in subject and technique, he took photos of Paris from a hot-air balloon, the first photos of their kind. In addition, he scoured the sewers and catacombs of the city, taking numerous photos, the first to be illuminated by a flash.

Academy Salons and Exhibitions

Royal academies of art were government-funded institutions that had a profound effect on the art that was produced during the 19th century. The academies held numerous exhibitions, or salons. The French Salon was an exhibit that featured works chosen by a jury made up of critics and collectors. Artists who were selected to show in the Salon usually had subsequent professional success. Artists whose work was rejected, however, were often deemed failures. The Salon was very competitive and aroused debate about traditional art, which was often reminiscent of Classical Greek and Roman art, versus modern art, which reflected contemporary times. Some artists, including the Realists, revolted against the restrictions of the Salon and Academy and developed their own styles.

Great Works of Realism

Gustave Courbet's *The Stone Breakers* (1849) was one of the major paintings that turned art down the path of Realism. The painting stood more than five feet (1.5 m) tall and eight and a half feet (2.6 m) wide, too large a piece, some said, for a subject as ugly as workers breaking stone. Courbet's inspiration for the painting came one day as he

FOLLOWING PAGES: Courbet painted two versions of *The Stone Breakers*; the larger piece was destroyed by a World War II bombing, but the smaller version (shown) survived.

Courbet was intrigued by the peasants' calm acceptance of their lot in life.

traveled in rural France. Alongside the road, two men chipped away at stones, breaking them down into small pieces to make pavement. The men's backbreaking work spoke of their poverty, and Courbet was inspired to portray their strife in a painting. He asked them to come to his studio to model for him. One of the men was young, the other old, and Courbet was struck with the thought that if one begins his life doing such labor, he will have to labor in the same way until the end of his life. Courbet was intrigued by the peasants' calm acceptance of their lot in life, and this became one of the themes of *The Stone Breakers*.

REALISM

ourbet painted the scene as he saw it. The faces of the men are hidden from view; only their backs are visible. They are absorbed in their dull, repetitive task. Rather than call attention to individual features, Courbet treats them as representatives of the common worker. The scale of the original painting shows Courbet's respect for ordinary peasants and his belief that they had a place in high art and, therefore, a place in society. The injustice of the lives of the peasants was inherent in the true-to-life depiction. When the painting was displayed at the 1850 Salon, many art critics derided not only the details of the peasants' tasks, which they considered improper for high art, but also Courbet's application of thick paint by a **palette knife**, which they considered careless. Others, though, felt that the thickness of the paint conveyed the ruggedness of the setting.

The Gleaners (1857), by Courbet's contemporary Jean-François Millet, holds a similar theme of the laboring worker. In the foreground of the painting, three female peasants glean, or gather, the leftover grain after the harvest. Behind them, a harvested field stretches to a rim of haystacks and cottages. In the distance, near the horizon, more peasants toil. Millet was meticulous in his details, emphasizing the dignity of this rural task and the people who performed it. The women toil, yet they do so with a certain amount of grandeur and pride. The colors of the painting are warm, and the hazy atmosphere creates a soothing effect, but the viewer is still aware that the subjects live in extreme poverty.

As in the case of Courbet's *The Stone Breakers*, Millet did not depict the figures as individuals but as **anonymous** members of the peasantry; he painted only their hunched

From 1849 until his death, Millet lived in a small village southeast of Paris called Barbizon. There, he helped foster the Barbizon school of art, which was concerned with Realism in landscape painting, and did some of his best work, such as *The Gleaners*.

bodies, with little attention to their faces. His intention was not to show the plight of the peasant. Instead, he wished to show that peasants and their daily tasks should be respected and admired. He was an avid reader of the Bible, and he believed that because of Adam and Eve's original sin, it was humanity's fate to toil and sweat in order to live. The peasants were to be praised because they accepted this fate without complaint.

Urban Paris was not without its working class, and *The Third-Class Carriage* (c. 1862), a painting by Honoré Daumier, provides a glimpse into the life of the city-dwelling poor. The scene of the painting is the interior of the third-class section of one of Paris's horse-drawn buses. The bus is crowded, and the passengers are tired and underprivileged. The painting focuses on a grandmother, her daughter, and her two grandchildren,

Millet wished to show that peasants and their daily tasks should be respected and admired.

all portrayed as they ordinarily appeared—unrehearsed and not posed for an observer. Though they are poor, the family members look content, serene, and intimate. In other sections of the bus, the riders are set apart from each other. One of Daumier's social concerns was that industrialization was causing individuals to become less intimate toward each other, and this theme appeared often in his work.

T

hree Women in Church (1878–82) is considered one of the greatest masterpieces of the Realist movement. Wilhelm Leibl spent more than three years in rural Bavaria working on the painting. He painted inside the village church depicted in the piece rather than in his studio. Often, it was so cold that his fingers grew stiff, and on some occasions, it was so dark that he had a difficult time seeing. The painting features a young woman in a church next to two older women, each of them reverent in prayer. The young woman is lovely and fresh, a contrast to the wrinkled faces of the two older women. This difference is emphasized by the dark background behind the young woman, which makes her face appear light, and the light background behind the older women, which makes their faces appear dark. The three women's

The Gustave Courbet Museum

The Gustave Courbet Museum is housed in the former residence of Gustave Courbet in the village of Ornans in eastern France. Visitors can browse more than 83 paintings, sculptures, and drawings by this master of the Realist movement. Pieces from all periods of Courbet's artistic career are featured, including his early paintings *Pirate, Prisoner of the Dey d'Alger* (1844) and *Rustic Hunters* (1857), and a piece from his later days called *The Castle at Chillon* (1874). In addition to Courbet's art, visitors can take in the hanging gardens and a beautiful view of the Loue River.

TAKEAWAY

"I have always set greater store by the opinion of simple peasants than by that of so-called painters."

—WILHELM LEIBL

devotion to their faith is evident by the calm patience radiating from their expressions. The dresses the women wear are simple and traditional, which shows that they haven't yet been affected by urban styles and trends. The painting is so powerful that while Leibl was working on it, several peasants stopped to look and instinctively folded their hands in prayer. Leibl was pleased by the reaction and wrote, "I have always set greater store by the opinion of simple peasants than by that of so-called painters."

An American painting, *The Gross Clinic* (1875), depicts a medical procedure performed by Dr. Samuel Gross at the Jefferson Medical College in Philadelphia. Thomas Eakins (1844–1916) painted the piece on **commission** from the college. He was chosen because of his interest in medical **anatomy** and also because he often attended Dr. Gross's medical lectures. In the painting, Dr. Gross is performing a surgery in the lecture hall of the college. He holds his scalpel with bloody hands as he lectures on the procedure. He is surrounded by his colleagues as well as by the patient's mother, who covers her face with her hands. The painting is unsparing in its re-creation of the event, and it was rejected for an 1876 Philadelphia art exhibition because of its gruesome detail.

Thomas Eakins took his artistic subjects directly from his life and made his work intensely autobiographical. Whether he was painting his family at home, his friends outdoors, or surgical procedures witnessed at a nearby medical college (such as *The Gross Clinic*), Eakins infused each work with rich, personal knowledge.

THE J. PAUL GETTY MUSEUM

The J. Paul Getty Museum

On a hilltop in the spectacular Santa Monica Mountains, the J. Paul Getty Museum at the Getty Center in Los Angeles, California, houses European paintings, drawings, sculpture, decorative arts, illuminated manuscripts—some of which date back to the ninth century A.D.—and European and American photographs. Visitors to the museum can view famous paintings from the years 1295 to 1895, including works of Realism such as Jean-François Millet's *Man with a Hoe* (1862), Gustave Courbet's *Grotto of Sarrazine near Nans-sous-Sainte-Anne* (1864), and many of Nadar's photographs. Outside, visitors can enjoy the Center Garden, designed by American artist Robert Irwin.

African American painter Henry Ossawa Tanner (1859–1937) was a student of Eakins's who had success in depicting Realist subjects and, later in life, religious subjects. After studying under Eakins, Tanner went to Paris. Upon his return, he shifted his interest to portraying the life of African Americans in his art. *The Thankful Poor* (1894) shows an elderly man and a young boy sitting at a table, praying. The painting reflects Tanner's past as the son of a minister, and it is evident that he regards his subjects with respect. Light streaming across the wall illuminates the pair. Deep shadows on the brow of the old man show his concentration on his worship. The man and the boy are the detailed focus of the piece; the rest of the painting is soft and almost blurred with loose strokes of color. With his paintings of African Americans, Tanner wanted to show the serious side of their lives rather than the comic **stereotype** of African Americans that prevailed at the time.

The foundation of Realist doctrine was that fact took precedence over fiction.

The Transformation of Realism

Although the Realist movement was dominant through the end of the 19th century, not all artists followed its philosophies. The foundation of Realist doctrine was that fact took precedence over fiction and was the basis of artistic truth and personal honesty, but some artists felt that this doctrine was too restrictive and did not allow enough room for imagination. These artists melded Realism with other styles and ideas, allowing them to adhere to the Realist techniques of portraying truthful detail while also using imaginative subjects.

ne such group of artists was the Pre-Raphaelite Brotherhood, which included John Everett Millais (1829–96) and Dante Gabriel Rossetti (1828–82). These artists wished to defy the principles and practices of British art at the time, which they felt had been misguided since the age of Italian Renaissance

painter Raphael (1483–1520). They believed that the unnatural, highly posed compositions of Raphael and his followers had led to formula-driven, academic art. In its place, the Pre-Raphaelites admired the natural, realistic styles of early northern European Renaissance masters, such as Albrecht Dürer (1471–1528) of Germany and Jan van Eyck (c. 1370–1440) of Belgium, and wished to combine Realism with a moral approach to art. Although they used Realistic styles in their artwork, the Pre-Raphaelites refused to be confined to contemporary life as subject matter. Instead, they had a fascination for the medieval period, and many of their paintings were of medieval subjects, such as Guinevere of King Arthur's court, painted in a Realistic manner.

Even as these changes were taking place within the Realist movement, changes in the outside world also

 REALISM

began to have an effect on Realism. As many European countries established and retained colonies in lands such as India, Africa, and the Americas during the 19th century, European cultural influence spread to nearly all corners of the globe, and faraway customs were introduced to Europe, changing many views on art and culture. Trade increased between Europe and Asia, and by the 1870s, Japanese art and cultural objects such as woodblock prints, perfumes, fans, and other decorative items had become popular with Europeans. The eye of the artist as well as the patron looked away from Realism and toward a more exotic style.

In addition, by the last half of the 19th century, though the gap between the upper and working classes was still wide, the conflict between the classes had eased, in part due to scientific innovations and discoveries that

European cultural influence spread to nearly all corners of the globe, and faraway customs were introduced to Europe.

increased the quality of life for many, both rich and poor. In 1864, the experiments of French chemist Louis Pasteur (1822–95) confirmed the theory that disease was spread by germs, and Pasteur and other scientists went on to develop vaccines and promote public sanitation and national disease control. The prospect of longer life spans energized the public. Although many problems remained in the lives of the working class, their futures did not seem as dire as before, and public, as well as artistic, attention shifted from their plight as the middle class experienced rapid growth.

 REALISM

By the 1860s, the upper middle class had a strong hold on political policy and societal trends, and in France, artists were turning away from common people as subject matter and toward the upper middle class, the city, and **leisure**. One artist, Edouard Manet (1832–83), was an important bridge between Realism and the following movement of Impressionism. Manet was a Realist who wanted to capture the passing moment. His painting *Luncheon on the Grass* (1863) was a highly **controversial** piece that was a turning point for Realist art. In this piece, two fully clothed men sit near two women, one of whom is nude and the other of whom is scantily dressed. Remnants of their picnic lie on the grass near them. The men are engaged in conversation and appear indifferent toward the first woman's nakedness, and the woman herself looks unbothered. The piece's casual nudity was not its only controversial aspect, however. Manet painted the picture with spontaneous brushstrokes that were meant to capture the light of the scene rather than the lines. The paint itself, not what it portrayed or stood for, was Manet's primary focus. Critics dismissed the painting as too sketch-like and informal, but today the piece is considered to be the gateway to modern ideas about art.

any French painters took Manet's spontaneous, light-influenced method one step far-

Edouard Manet took the inspiration for his *Luncheon on the Grass* from Classical subject matter but shocked his Parisian audience with his startlingly modern and realistic interpretation. What many saw was a present-day scandal represented in garish full color.

ther to a style that became known as Impressionism. The Impressionist movement marked the shift toward modern and **abstract art.** As the Realists had before them, Impressionists painted scenes from daily life. Unlike the Realists, however, Impressionists focused on the upper middle class rather than the working class. The focus of Realism on the lifestyles of the common people allowed Impressionist artists the freedom to draw from the world around them rather than from history or Classical models.

Unlike the Realists, Whistler believed that art should be a cure for the ugliness of modern life.

In America, artists such as James McNeill Whistler (1834–1903) began to move away from Realism as well. Although Whistler's **etching** *Black Lion Wharf* (1859) features a realistic setting inspired by Gustave Courbet, Whistler did not adhere to Courbet's ideas about composition or the social aspect of art. Courbet's pieces have a firm central focus, but *Black Lion Wharf* is horizontal and has no strong focal point, causing the viewer to scan the piece quickly. As his ideas about Realism changed, Whistler moved to London to escape the influence of Courbet. Unlike the Realists, Whistler believed that art should be a cure for the ugliness of modern life. This idea became the founding principle for Aestheticism, a movement that reached the height of its popularity in Europe in the 1880s. Aesthetes believed that art should not serve a moral or social purpose;

rather, it existed solely to be beautiful. Aestheticism was widely a reaction against Realism and rejected Realist subjects of contemporary life, which were ordinary and unremarkable, in favor of images that were beautiful and pleasing to the eye.

Although some American artists such as Whistler began to turn away from Realism in the late 19th century, others, including a small group of New York City artists known as the Ashcan School, continued to paint in the Realist style into the 20th century.

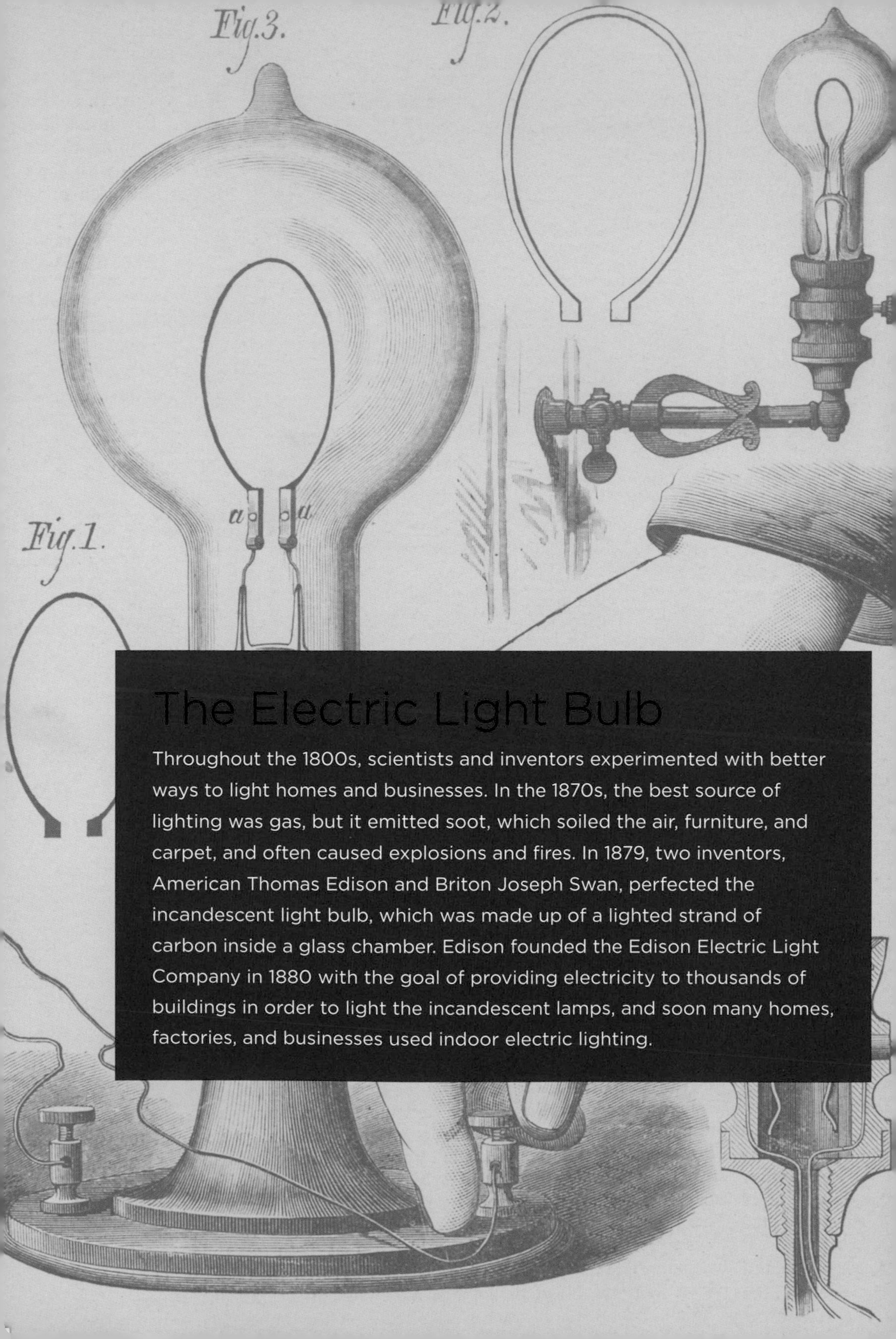

Fig.3.

Fig.2.

Fig.1.

The Electric Light Bulb

Throughout the 1800s, scientists and inventors experimented with better ways to light homes and businesses. In the 1870s, the best source of lighting was gas, but it emitted soot, which soiled the air, furniture, and carpet, and often caused explosions and fires. In 1879, two inventors, American Thomas Edison and Briton Joseph Swan, perfected the incandescent light bulb, which was made up of a lighted strand of carbon inside a glass chamber. Edison founded the Edison Electric Light Company in 1880 with the goal of providing electricity to thousands of buildings in order to light the incandescent lamps, and soon many homes, factories, and businesses used indoor electric lighting.

Comprising eight artists at first, the most prominent being Robert Henri (1865–1929), the Ashcan School was known for paintings that portrayed scenes of daily life in poor urban America from the years 1908 to 1920. Many of the themes that had characterized the 19th century Realist movement were prevalent in the work of the Ashcan School of artists as well.

The Realist movement illuminated the plight of the common people, erasing preconceived ideas about proper subject matter in art and redrawing the boundaries to include the poor and the working class. A true and accurate account of the world around them was the Realists' goal, and to obtain this goal, they often had to delve into places the art world had never seen—sometimes using new methods such as photography—to bring the world of the 19th century from the dark into the light.

The Musée d'Orsay

The Musée d'Orsay in Paris showcases works of photography, architecture, painting, sculpture, and graphic arts from the period 1848 to 1914, including a large collection of Realist art. Paintings such as Gustave Courbet's *Burial at Ornans* (1849–50), Rosa Bonheur's *The Horse Fair*, and Edouard Manet's *Luncheon on the Grass* are housed in the museum's many corridors. Visitors can also examine the artwork of many other significant movements of the 19th and 20th centuries, including Symbolism and Impressionism, and enjoy the architecture of the museum, which was once a train station.

Timeline

1804   The first steam locomotive is completed and operated

1814   Francis Cabot Lowell establishes one of the first textile mills in the U.S.

1815   Napoleon I falls from power in France

1839   The daguerreotype method of photography is released to the public

1844   William Henry Fox Talbot publishes the first book illustrated with photographs, *The Pencil of Nature*

1846   Belgian Adolphe Sax patents the saxophone and creates a line of single-reed woodwinds, including the clarinet

1848   Karl Marx and Friedrich Engels publish *The Communist Manifesto*, and socialist revolutions erupt in Paris and other major cities

1849   A movement known as *Verismo* (Realism) begins in Italy

1850   Gustave Courbet shows *The Stone Breakers*, *Burial at Ornans*, and *Peasants of Flagey* at the Paris Salon

1852   Napoleon III is declared emperor of France

1853   Nadar opens a portrait studio in Paris

1855   Courbet sets up the Pavilion of Realism near the Universal Exhibition of 1855 in Paris

1857   Jean-François Millet paints *The Gleaners*

1858   Plans are laid for Central Park in New York City

1861   The American Civil War begins

1862   Honoré Daumier paints *The Third-Class Carriage*

1863   President Lincoln issues the Emancipation Proclamation,
        which frees slaves in the southern U.S.; Edouard Manet
        exhibits *Luncheon on the Grass*

1865   The Southern Confederacy surrenders to the North,
        ending the American Civil War

1871   France is defeated in the Franco-Prussian War

1875   Thomas Eakins paints *The Gross Clinic*

Bibliography

Cole, Bruce, and Adelheid Gealt. *Art of the Western World:
    From Ancient Greece to Post-Modernism*. New York: Simon
    & Schuster, 1989.

Gardner, Louise. *Art through the Ages*. Orlando, Fla.: Harcourt
    Brace, 1991.

Gilbert, Rita, and William McCarter. *Living with Art*. 2nd ed.
    New York: Knopf, 1985.

Nochlin, Linda. *Realism and Tradition in Art: 1848–1900*.
    Englewood, N.J.: Prentice-Hall, 1966.

Rosen, Charles, and Henri Zerner. *Romanticism and Realism:
    The Mythology of Nineteenth Century Art*. New York: Viking
    Press, 1984.

Young, Nahonri Sharp. *The Eight: The Realist Revolt in
    American Painting*. New York: Watson-Guptill, 1973.

Glossary

abstract art   art with images that do not represent the physical truth of objects

academic   conforming to the rules of an academy, or society of scholars or artists, such as the Royal Academy of Painting and Sculpture in France

anatomy   the scientific study of the structure of a living thing, especially the human body

anonymous   having an unknown name or identity

commission   money paid for special work done

controversial   causing much argument or debate

democratic   having to do with a system of government in which leaders are elected by the people

economic   having to do with the way money, goods, and services affect a society

etching   a picture or print made from an engraved plate; the engraving is done on metal or glass using a sharp object and acid to cut through the surface

Industrial Revolution   a period of time from the mid-1700s to the early 1900s in which machines replaced work done by hand and new methods of transportation were developed

iodized   treated with the element iodine